FOOTPRINTS OF WELLNESS

ONE STEP AHEAD: MANAGING DIABETIC FOOT HEALTH

DR. FIRDOUS SHAIKH

To my cherished teacher, the **Late Dr. Suresh Mehtalia,** Who graced this world for 89 remarkable years and dedicated nearly 40 of them to the honorable and noble profession of teaching and saving countless lives. Your presence has contributed to my identity as well as to my academic trajectory.

Your unwavering love, dedication, and optimism for your patients and students are unmatched. Even though you are no longer among us, the principles and lessons you taught will have an everlasting impact on the lives you touched, especially your students. This book is my small homage to your enduring legacy, which will live on in the hearts of all those who had the privilege of learning and healing from you.

Honoring Dr. Suresh Mehtalia Sir at Nehru Art Gallery during my first exhibition.

Contents

Preface

"The feet that bow in humility carry the soul to the divine."

One busy morning during the festive season, my 40-year-old patient, *Mrs.Bhavna** (name changed) visited my clinic in Bandra. She looked tired and distressed as she explained her condition. Because of her long-standing diabetes, her feet were not in good shape and she could no longer bend down to touch the feet of elders during festivals. This simple act, known as *"Charan Sparsh"*is a deeply respected tradition in India, especially during occasions like Diwali.

That day, I understood something very important. In our country, India, diabetes doesn't just describe a medical condition—it shapes the way people exist, pray, celebrate, and connect with their families, friends, faith, and traditions. This moment inspired me to write this book, combining medical knowledge with the cultural and spiritual challenges faced by people with diabetes in our country.

As a diabetologist, I have witnessed firsthand how one silent assault of diabetes, called **peripheral neuropathy** (a condition that affects the nerves of the hands and feet, causing severe pain, tingling, or numbness) is often disregarded by many. My initiation into understanding and advocating for foot care started with the heart-wrenching patient stories that stemmed from ignorance.

This book is an amalgamation of my experiences, and it is my hope to create a future where no one loses their steps to diabetes.

Foreword

Dr Vijay Viswanathan - MD PhD FRCP (President RSSDI)Honorary President and Board member D - Foot International Belgium,Hon Gen Secretary Association of Physicians of India Chennai

I introduce "**Footprints of Wellness**" with great pleasure and a deep sense of responsibility. This remarkable book by Dr Firdous Shaikh sheds light on an often-overlooked aspect of diabetes care, the profound connection between our feet, health, and everyday lives.

Diabetes is a growing global challenge, touching every community and affecting countless lives. Amid the clinical focus on managing blood sugar levels, the critical role of foot care is frequently underestimated. Yet, for those living with diabetes, proper foot health can mean the difference between wellness and quality of life. This book combines science, culture, and personal empowerment to address this essential topic.

The chapters are thoughtfully designed, weaving together knowledge and practicality. Beginning with a solid foundation in understanding diabetes and its impact on foot health, the book invites readers to take "mindful steps" toward a better life. The authors draw from diverse sources of wisdom—traditional practices, modern therapies, community engagement, and even cultural rituals—to create a comprehensive guide. By placing equal emphasis on physical, emotional, and social well-being, this book not only informs but inspires.

Whether you are a healthcare provider, a caregiver, or someone living with diabetes, this book is a must-read. It empowers you to take charge of your health and become an advocate for wellness within your family and community.

As we turn to the future of diabetes care, "Footprints of Wellness" serves as a roadmap of hope. May its words inspire steps of faith, action, and care—leaving behind footprints that guide us toward a healthier tomorrow.

Best Wishes,
Dr Vijay Viswanathan

Foreword – 2

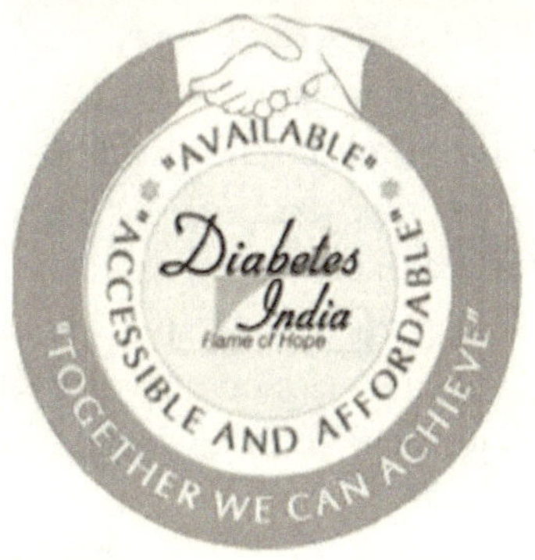

Dr. Banshi Saboo MD, FIACM, FICN, FACE, MNAMSChair-Elect for the International Diabetes Federation (IDF), Honorary Secretary of Diabetes India, Honorary Vice President of Diabetes in Asia Study Group

It is with immense pleasure and admiration that I pen this foreword for "**Footprints of Wellness**" by Dr. Firdous Shaikh. I deeply appreciate the thoughtfulness this book embodies. Dr. Shaikh has skilfully highlighted an often-overlooked aspect of diabetes management: foot health, intertwining medical insights with the rich tapestry of cultural and spiritual values prevalent in our society.

The diabetic foot is a silent yet significant battleground in the fight against diabetes. It reflects how diabetes, beyond its physiological impacts, deeply influences one's quality of life, mobility, and social connections. Through real-life patient stories and practical advice, Dr. Shaikh has artfully conveyed the profound challenges individuals face and provided actionable solutions to overcome them.

What makes this book unique is its holistic approach. By integrating traditional practices with modern medical science, Dr. Shaikh bridges the gap between cultural heritage and evidence-based care. Whether it is guiding a patient on performing religious rituals safely or offering advice on selecting diabetic-friendly footwear, this book is a comprehensive resource for anyone living with diabetes, their caregivers, and healthcare providers alike.

In a time when diabetes is on the rise globally, this work serves as a beacon of hope and empowerment. It reminds us that managing diabetes is not merely about controlling blood glucose levels but about embracing a lifestyle of self-care, education, and cultural understanding. Dr. Shaikh's passion and dedication shine through every chapter, making this book an invaluable tool for transforming lives.

I wholeheartedly congratulate Dr. Firdous Shaikh on this remarkable achievement and encourage readers to take inspiration from the knowledge and compassion embedded within these pages. Together, let us take mindful steps toward wellness and ensure that no one loses their footing in their journey to a healthier life.

Best Wishes,

Dr. Banshi Saboo

Foreword - 3

Dr . Manoj ChawlaDirector and Consultant Diabetologist at Lina Diabetes Care & Mumbai Diabetes Research CentreMember of the Maharashtra Medical Council, India representative at IDF General Assembly,Central RSSDI EC Member

It gives me immense pleasure to write this foreword for this insightful book on **"Footprints Of Wellness"** byDr. Firdous Shaikh. Drawing from her learnings and experiences, Dr. Firdous has skillfully crafted a resource that is both simple and practical, addressing a critical yet often overlooked aspect of diabetes care.

Diabetic foot complications continue to pose a mammoth challenge in India, largely due to cultural beliefs and traditional practices such as walking barefoot. These factors, coupled with the growing prevalence of diabetes, make awareness and education about foot care indispensable. Dr. Firdous has taken a commendable step in bridging this gap by sharing her clinical wisdom and observations in a manner that will undoubtedly resonate with readers and patients alike.

I congratulate Dr. Firdous Shaikh on her dedication and efforts in producing this book, which I believe will serve as a valuable guide for both patients and healthcare providers. I wish her continued success in her journey as a diabetologist and encourage her to further enrich her clinical knowledge and share her insights to benefit many more lives.

To the readers, I wish you a joyful and informative reading experience. May this book inspire better understanding and proactive care for diabetic foot health.

With best wishes,
Dr. Manoj Chawla

Acknowledgements

To my **Mother,** who taught me that medicine begins with the heart and healing starts with compassion. Your nurturing spirit has shown me that being a good doctor means being a good human first. Mere words of thanks can never fully capture my gratitude for the lifetime of lessons you have given me and continue to bestow. Your unwavering love and guidance are the foundation of all that I am and aspire to be.

I am incredibly grateful and deeply indebted to my teachers—**Dr. Manoj Chawla, Dr. Jasmina Vora, Dr. Anil Bhoraskar**, and the **Late Dr. Suresh Mehtalia**—whose guidance forms the foundation of my journey. Each of them, in their unique style, has taught me lessons that extend far beyond the realm of medicine, shaping not only my professional path but also preparing and moulding me to face the real world.

Dr. Manoj Chawla's unwavering mentorship taught me the importance of perseverance and innovation in advancing diabetes care. Dr. Jasmina Vora's firm yet tender guidance emphasized the value of compassion and precision in patient care. Dr. Anil Bhoraskar's quick thinking, confidence, and witty humour have taught me how to truly live, enjoy life, and embrace my profession while differentiating between the real and reel world. And the Late Dr. Suresh Mehtalia, with his timeless legacy, instilled in me the deeper purpose of medicine—to heal not just bodies but also lives.

Their collective knowledge, wisdom, and dedication to this noble profession have inspired me to embrace the true significance of healing with empathy and integrity.

ACKNOWLEDGEMENTS

Dr. Manoj Chawla

Dr. Jasmina Vora

Dr. Anil Bhoraskar

Dr. Suresh Mehtalia

UNDERSTANDING DIABETES AND FOOT PROBLEMS

"The greatest step you can take towards health is the one that keeps your feet on the ground."
— Anonymous

In today's modern world, many look at diabetes as one of those minor health conditions that can be treated with just a couple of medications. This, however, I must say as a doctor, is far from the truth. Diabetes takes away your whole life; silent and cunning as it may be, it is far more than a *minor hassle*.

It slowly infiltrates the body, silently harming systems and organs, without the patient even realizing the magnitude of the threat they are facing. As a doctor, I feel privileged to dedicate my life to learning about and preventing this complex disease, but I am also very concerned about the number of people who are unaware of the serious consequences diabetes can have on their bodies, especially with regard to the feet. Diabetes is a complex disease that causes several complications, to name a few: peripheral nerve damage, poor circulatory conditions, infections, and, in more severe conditions, *amputation (surgically removing a part of the body due to serious infection)* if neglected.

What is Diabetes?

Diabetes is a long term condition that interferes with the body's natural ability to regulate blood sugar levels. This occurs either because the body can't produce enough insulin or because it becomes resistant to insulin. Think of insulin as a key that unlocks cells, allowing them to absorb sugar from the bloodstream and convert it into energy. However, in diabetes, this system breaks down in one of two ways: either the body stops producing enough insulin or the cells become resistant to insulin's effects.

In this case, sugar builds up in the bloodstream instead of entering cells where it belongs. Without insulin, or when the body is unable to utilize it correctly, blood sugar levels rise, potentially causing many dangerous complications. Diabetes can be devastatingly destructive to most organs of the body: heart, kidneys, eyes, and nerves. This condition is not only physical; it impairs the mental and emotional well-being of a person and their ability to indulge in the most fundamental and cherished activities of life.

How does Diabetes affect the feet?

Diabetes can have a devastating effect on the feet. Poor circulation and diabetic neuropathy (damage to the nerves) can cause even minor foot problems to rapidly escalate into life-threatening conditions. *Diabetes is the world's leading cause of lower limb amputations*, and with the right care and attention, a substantial percentage of such cases can be prevented.

When nerves in the feet are damaged due to high blood sugar levels, people lose sensation in their feet. This means that cuts, blisters, or even infections may go unnoticed until they become severe. The lack of sensation, combined with poor blood flow, makes it more difficult for the body to heal injuries, leading to a higher risk of infection and, ultimately, amputation. It is not just about the feet; it is about a person's ability to live their life as they did before. From walking and running to simply standing or sitting comfortably, diabetes-related foot problems affect everything. Diabetes doesn't just change the way people live—it changes the way they experience the world. The feet, which are often taken for granted, become the battleground in this fight against a chronic and life-altering disease.

There are several types of foot problems that people with diabetes may face:

<u>Diabetic Neuropathy:</u>This condition happens when high blood sugar levels over time damage the nerves of the hands and feet, causing pain, discomfort, tingling sensation, or even numbness. Because of reduced sensation, injuries may go unnoticed, which can lead to more serious complications.

<u>Poor Circulation:</u> Diabetes causes compromised blood flow. If blood flow to the feet is decreased, infections or wounds may take a longer time to heal and may even result in serious infections in extreme cases leading to gangrene (*a medical emergency where skin turns black and tissues die due to poor blood flow and infection*)

<u>Foot Ulcers:</u> Diabetic patients may develop open wounds or ulcers on their feet. Due to nerve damage and poor circulation, early signs often go unnoticed, leading to infections. If not treated, these ulcers can become severe and may even require amputation.

<u>Infections:</u>Diabetes weakens the immune system and slows down the healing process. Even small cuts or blisters can become quickly infected. It's important for people with diabetes to keep their feet clean and take good care of them to avoid infections especially between the toe spaces.

<u>Charcot Foot:</u> Charcot Foot is a progressive condition caused by nerve damage and weak bones in the foot and ankle of people with long-standing diabetes. The joint becomes swollen and appears larger than usual. The bones shift out of position, and small pieces of bone and cartilage may become dislodged inside the joint. The bones around the joint become harder and denser, causing continued damage to the joint.

It is crucial for people with diabetes to maintain proper foot hygiene to prevent infections.

CHAPTER TWO

SACRED STEPS

"In every step, there is a story—of love, faith, and family. When diabetes dims that light, we lose more than just the ability to walk; we lose our connection to life itself."– Anonymous

Indian rituals are more than just customs; they are a means of achieving spirituality and establishing a heavenly bond that permeates everyday existence. This chapter looks at the importance of feet in Indian culture, how they relate to health, and how modern medicine might complement traditional customs to provide comprehensive remedies. Feet represent dedication, humility, respect, and mobility in Indian culture.

Touching the feet of elders remains a deeply respected custom in India even today. This ancient practice goes beyond reverence, it establishes a bond between generations while seeking blessings from those who have walked life's path before us. Indians have long understood the significance of feet, not just as a symbol of mobility and respect, but as foundations of well-being. From the cool marble floors of temples, mosques, and churches, to the warm earth of village courtyards, feet connect the physical and spiritual realms of Indian life, bridging the gap between tradition and health.

I met *Rekha Aunty* *(name changed) one morning in my clinic in Bandra, a peaceful Mumbai suburb. Her personal tale touched my heart. She had been performing morning puja every day for sixty years, sitting cross-legged in front of her home shrine in prayer and divine interaction. Her everyday activities were not disturbed by her medical condition over the previous twenty years, but at seventy-five, the negative impacts of diabetes were causing a hindrance in her routine as she could no longer sit cross-legged due to the severe aches and pain that had been gradually encroaching on her feet over the past three months, endangering a lifetime of spiritual connection.

Her diminishing voice revealed deep sadness. Despite the fact that I dealt with numerous cases of neuropathy, *Rekha Aunty* said something that struck an emotional chord in me. In addition to affecting her physical health, her spiritual relationship with the divine was also affected due to diabetes. This loss, which cannot be measured by blood sugar levels or numbers, led me to realize that diabetes impairs not only physical health but also the core being of who we are.

I recall using a relatable analogy to *Rekha Aunty* to explain neuropathy: "Think of neuropathy as the wiring of a lamp. If the wiring becomes damaged, the light bulb doesn't receive the power it needs to glow." Similarly, when diabetes keeps your blood sugar levels high for too long, it's like constant power surges damaging those wires. Eventually, the signals - in this case, your nerves are getting damaged because of the long duration of diabetes causing the burning and painful sensation in your feet." Her eyes gleamed with comprehension, but the challenge still stood! How could I support her in continuing her spiritual activities while preserving her physical health too. *Rekha Aunty's* story is not uncommon. Many people with diabetes experience similar challenges with their feet.

After hearing her "waning voice", I thought: what if the issue could be resolved on both a spiritual and physical level? What if tradition and science could merge together to offer a solution that respected both.

In order to figure out a solution, I firstly counseled her to avoid sitting cross- legged for lengthy periods. Secondly, I asked her to get a custom-made cushioned stool that positioned her at an appropriate height for her shrine so that she could sit comfortably in an elevated position which would decrease the strain on her feet.

I then revised her current treatment regimen and counseled her again about the importance of adhering to medications and following a proper diet plan which would address both her medical and spiritual needs.

However, for people with diabetes, these traditions can become challenging when foot problems arise. *Rekha Aunty's* case is just one of many such cases that people with diabetes face. But it doesn't have to be this way. By making small adjustments, it's possible to restore both the physical and spiritual ties that diabetes threatens to break.

Modifying the way we perform religious rituals can make a huge difference. After seeking medical advice, *Rekha Aunty* started using a cushioned stool for her puja. Instead of sitting cross-legged, she sat comfortably on the stool and performed her prayers without straining her feet. This simple adjustment allowed her to continue her connection to the divine without discomfort.

It might be challenging for many people living with diabetes to balance their duties while taking good care of their feet. One such patient, a temple priest narrated his condition which prompted him to change his way of life. He was able to continue working by using orthotic shoes and taking care of his feet. His story demonstrates that prioritizing foot health while upholding cultural and spiritual traditions is feasible with the correct assistance. The significance of feet in numerous religious traditions around the world is astounding. It is easy to understand how the ancient Christian custom of washing one's feet represents humility. This highlights the importance of foot health and how many people with diabetes may continue to have vibrant lives within the framework of their belief system.

The amalgamation of medicine and tradition offers significant solutions. This chapter reminds us that although modern medicine is vital, we also need to respect the deeply ingrained customs that give us a feeling of identity and tranquility.

We learned from *Rekha Aunty's* journey that the sanctity of everyday rituals need not be compromised by diabetes. Rather, with the correct information and resources, we can improve, maintain, and enhance our spiritual and physical well-being.

Important Foot Care Tips from *Rekha Aunty's* Experience:

<u>Examine Your Feet Daily</u>

Why: The key to avoiding problems is early detection of wounds, blisters, or infections.

How: Examine your feet daily. Use a mirror or ask a loved one for assistance if needed.

<u>Moisturize Your Skin:</u>

Why: Cracked, dry skin can serve as a point of entry for infections.

What to do: Moisturize your skin daily, avoiding the spaces between your toes to decrease the risk of fungal infections.

<u>Improve Blood circulation:</u>

Why: Diabetes-related foot problems are frequently exacerbated by poor blood circulation.

What to do: Avoid sitting cross-legged for long periods. While seated, raise your feet and perform foot exercises such as ankle rotations and toe wiggling

<u>Reduce Pressure on Your feet:</u>

Why: Constant pressure might worsen neuropathy and cause ulcers.

What to do: Use diabetic - friendly footwear. Use cushioned stools if seated for prolonged periods. Switch between standing and sitting positions whenever possible.

<u>Maintain good blood sugar control:</u>

Why: Good blood sugar control prevents complications like nerve damage and promotes healing and reduces chances of infections.

What to do: Take your diabetes medications daily as advised by your doctor.

<u>Regular Health Check-up:</u>

Why: Regular health examinations aid in early identification of problems.

What to do: Schedule regular appointments and follow up diligently with your diabetologist and podiatrist(Foot care specialist).

CHAPTER THREE

STEPS OF FAITH

"Spirituality does not demand suffering; it invites balance. When we take care of our body, we honor our soul's connection with the divine."- Anonymous

Here's another gripping case of my patient *Mr. Irfan** (name changed), a devoted Muslim whose unshakable faith was put to the test by physical adversity. This kindhearted man longed to continue performing his five daily prayers, despite excruciating pain in his legs. The agony of the pain grew harder and harder for him to stand, kneel, and sit during Namaaz. *Mr. Irfan* initially had no intention of altering his prayer routine. He thought it would be improper to change the way he prayed. However, after thorough counseling and reassuring him that the changes adviced in his prayer routine would not affect his connection with the divine as every religion teaches us to respect our health and not cause undue suffering. He then agreed to find a middle path and sit on a chair and offer his daily prayers as the pain in his feet was becoming increasingly intolerable.

His treatment regimen was also modified to include insulin therapy, as oral medications alone would not suffice to control his sugars effectively and quickly. He held the misconception that once insulin was initiated, it would need to be taken lifelong — a common myth many people in India believe. Despite his reluctance, and addressing his misconception, that insulin therapy is only a temporary measure until his blood sugars come under control, he hesitantly agreed. After a month of this minor adjustment and change in his medication regimen, he was extremely joyous as his pain reduced and his blood sugar levels also improved, most importantly his misconception about insulin use were cleared and with this newfound knowledge he began counseling other's. He was adviced to use a special prayer mat with more cushioning at that point. This adjustment again had a significant impact. The soft prayer mat helped reduce the pressure on his feet, making it easier for him to kneel and sit during his prayers. By complying with my advice and having faith in me, he was able to pray in the original technique. His case teaches us that India, being a multicultural and multi-religious country, requires doctors to have knowledge of various religions and also dispelling myths people hold about diabetes management especially when it comes to use of Insulin. By giving extra time to counsel our patients better, not only makes them feel more comfortable and compliant to our advice but also empowers them to educate others and dispel myths thereby creating a positive ripple effect and building a more knowledgeable community.

Mr.Irfan additionally was taught proper wudu (ablution) techniques that are part of the prayer routine. He was taught more hygienic ways to wash his feet and pat them dry thoroughly to avoid fungal infections.

Another interesting part of this chapter is looking at how people take care of their feet during pilgrimages. Pilgrimages like the journey to **Amarnath** or **Hajj** in Saudi Arabia require a lot of walking, sometimes for miles, which can be hard on the feet. One such case that stands out is that of my elderly patient *Mr.Mehta** (name changed) who went on Amarnath Yatra despite his age and diabetes. He took special care of his feet, using cushioned shoes, resting when needed, and checking his feet regularly for any sores or blisters. His story is a reminder that with the right care, even long and difficult journeys can be completed safely. **"Age is just a number if we take good care of our health"**.

Through these cases and examples, we see how important it is to treat our body with respect while practicing our faith. "*Mr. Irfan* and *Mr. Mehtas* journey teaches us" that with some adjustments and attention, we can continue our spiritual practices while taking care of our health, especially our feet. Whether it's during prayer, meditation, pilgrimage, or fasting, taking care of our feet is essential to staying healthy and connected to our spiritual well-being.

Tips to Manage Foot Care During Prayer and Religious Pilgrimage:

<u>Modified Prayer Postures:</u> While it's important to follow the traditional prayer postures, *Mr.Irfan* found that sitting on a chair during some parts of his prayers, instead of kneeling, helped relieve the pressure on his legs and feet.

<u>Use a Cushioned Prayer Mat:</u>Use a prayer mat with extra cushioning to add comfort while kneeling and sitting during prayers without experiencing much pain.

<u>Wudu (Ablution) Modifications:</u> Diabetic neuropathy increases the risk of infections in the feet, hence adopting proper techniques like washing the feet gently in between toe spaces with lukewarm water and dry them thoroughly to avoid fungal infections.

<u>Right diabetic footwear when going on pilgrimage:</u>Choose diabetic-friendly shoes with proper arch support and cushioning. These shoes help reduce pressure on your feet, preventing problems like sores, blisters, or calluses. Always check your shoes for any rough edges that may hurt your feet.

<u>Take breaks during long services:</u> If you're standing, walking, or sitting in any position for a long period of time time during prayer or religious services, make sure to take regular breaks and alternate those positions. Elevate your feet to improve circulation and relieve pressure.

<u>Inspect your feet regularly:</u>People with diabetes should check their feet every day for any cuts, blisters, or infections. If you find anything unusual, consult your doctor immediately. Early detection can prevent serious problems from developing.

By making these small yet effective changes, you can continue your spiritual practices without putting your feet at risk. Remember, taking care of your feet is essential to staying healthy, and with the right precautions, you can keep practicing your faith while ensuring your feet remain pain-free.

CHAPTER FOUR

THE DAILY RITUAL OF CARE

"Obsessing over every step may control the moment, but trusting the journey of care heals the soul. Let courage guide your feet, not fear."- Anonymous

In this chapter we will look into how *Mr. Sandeep* *(name changed), a 60-year-old retired banker who was diagnosed with Type 2 diabetes mellitus nearly two decades ago, developed a foot care ritual fueled by anxiety that became an element of control in his everyday life.

The event that triggered his fears and led to an obsession with checking his feet every day was after learning about an extended family member's toe being amputated as a consequence of poor blood sugar control which led to *gangrene, a condition when there is an inadequate blood supply which can lead to severe infections.* After hearing about this incident, *Mr. Sandeep* would frequently test tactile sensations, take meticulous pictures of his feet, and document any minor changes.

Despite having well-controlled diabetes, his nervousness caused him to avoid social gatherings and led to an obsessive pattern of checking his feet every morning for nearly an hour. During his follow-up appointment, I reassured him that his blood sugar levels were under very good control and that there were no warning signs of any complications with his feet. However, sensing that his fears were affecting his psychological well-being, I encouraged him to consult a mental health professional to help him deal with his fears and eliminate his habitual actions.

We devised a personalized treatment plan keeping in mind his psychiatric medications, some of which tend to increase blood sugar levels while also making some changes in his diabetic treatment regimen that would help control his sugars better. He was taught cognitive-behavioral skills to help manage his anxieties about complications from diabetes and helped him gain insight into the root causes of his compulsive behaviour.

Mr. Sandeep's case demonstrates the importance of addressing both the physical and psychological aspects of chronic disease management, particularly in diabetes care where anxiety about complications can significantly impact quality of life. Another important aspect we learn from this case is medical specialities must work in cohesion to provide holistic treatment.

Key Takeaway points from Mr. Sandeep's case:

- Check your feet once daily
- Maintain good blood glucose control
- Use diabetic- friendly footwear
- Exercise daily
- Regular consultation with your diabetologist, podiatrist and psychologist/psychiatrist
- Share your concerns with your doctor
- Community and Family support is important
- Recognize signs of anxiety or compulsive behaviour
- Practice relaxation techniques like deep breathing , yoga or journaling down your fears
- Join diabetes support groups to learn and share your experience and also for encouragement
- Avoid googling your symptoms and self- diagnosis, strictly seek professional help.

CHAPTER FIVE

FESTIVALS AND FOOT CARE

"Each festival is a chapter of joy and devotion, and with every step we safeguard, we write a story of health and happiness for ourselves and our loved ones."- Anonymous

Festivals in India are a time for rejoicing, devotion, and social gatherings. Every occasion for *The Gupta's* * (name changed) was about more than just following the rites and rituals - it was also about safeguarding their health while enjoying these treasured customs. This chapter follows their journey throughout the year to show how they embraced every festival without compromising on foot care.

Mrs.Gupta's Diwali:

Diwali, often known as the *Festival of Lights*, is a time for family get-togethers, fireworks, and happiness. But for *Mrs.Gupta*, Diwali used to come with its own unique challenges. One such year, while preparing for the festivities, she accidentally stepped on a broken diya and got a small cut on her foot. She realized that the festival's excitement and chaos could put her feet at risk of injury.

So, *Mrs.Gupta* started to wear comfortable shoes that gave her support while she was walking around the house . She also used secure diyas that had holders for stability so that there were fewer chances of any accidents occurring. These minor yet profound changes helped her enjoy the festival carefree.

Additionally, to promote a healthier lifestyle and enjoy the festivities she chose to make sugar-free sweets and confectioneries, setting an example for her family and neighbourhood, ensuring they could enjoy the festive treats without compromising their health.

Navratri and Foot Care:

Navratri is a festival dedicated to worshipping *Goddess Durga*, which involves fasting and dancing for nine-nights. For most people, this period is a fun-filled custom. However, foot pain was an unwelcome reality for *Mrs.Gupta's* daughter, *Priti,**(name changed) a 30-year old fashion designer who had been living with Type 1 diabetes for over 20 years. She often participated in the traditional dance known as *Garba*. After hours of joyful dancing, she would frequently develop blisters and have severe foot pain, dampering her enjoyment.

However, being a determined Type 1 warrior and extremely strong-willed, there was nothing that could stop her. *Priti* started wearing well-cushioned, customized and stylish, diabetic-friendly shoes that supported her feet while dancing to avoid getting painful blisters and discomfort during the event. Before the festival commenced, she additionally made sure that she got comfortable in her new shoes. Occasionally, she would soak her feet in lukewarm water after dancing, pat them dry thoroughly, and even get gentle massages. By taking all these precautions, *Priti* was able to dance through Navratri without any foot injuries.

Insights from a Wedding Season, Barefoot Ceremonies:

Indian marriages are immersed with traditions. In Hindu ceremonies, the bride and the groom are required to walk barefoot around the sacred fire, called the*Saat Phere*(seven rounds), which holds religious and cultural significance. Although these barefoot rituals hold significant spiritual meaning and importance, they can occasionally put the feet at risk for injuries, particularly when standing for extended periods of time or walking on hard and uneven surfaces.

Sneha *(name changed) was a bridesmaid for her friend's wedding. She was diagnosed with type 2 diabetes three years ago and also suffered from hypothyroidism (a condition in which the thyroid gland does not function adequately and produces fewer thyroid hormones). During this event, *Sneha* developed painful blisters from walking barefoot, on the rough and cold floor of the temple. Following this, *Sneha* avoided going barefoot and wore protective footwear both indoors and outdoors for subsequent wedding ceremonies. She applied moisturizer every night and gently massaged her feet to relieve soreness while also preventing dryness and cracking of the skin, which could be a source of infection. These simple precautions allowed her to participate in the ceremonies comfortably while safeguarding her foot health.

Christmas Celebrations, Midnight Mass, and Foot Health:

While Christmas is a season of joy, happiness, feasting and celebration, standing for extended periods of time during religious services, like midnight mass, can be hard on the feet. *Father Thomas** (name changed), a priest in Bandra, complained of tingling feeling and sporadic aches and pains in his feet. Even though he was quite diligent about his diabetes medications and food habits, the pain and tingling sensation were a consequence of his long-term diabetes. Due to this, he found it particularly challenging to stand for long hours while delivering sermons to his congregation. *Father Thomas* wasn't the only person who had this complaint; many people who go to midnight mass, particularly the elderly with diabetes, experience the same discomfort when standing for prolonged periods.

Father Thomas addressed his issue by switching to diabetic-friendly shoes that had good arch support and an extra layer of cushioning. During services, he began incorporating subtle foot and leg stretches, and he encouraged his congregation to do the same. His ministry expanded beyond spiritual guidance - alongside his religious teachings, he began counselling his congregation, particularly the younger population, about the importance of health. He emphasized eating a well-balanced diet, counseled against excessive consumption of processed foods, promoted physical activities while also particularly emphasizing on not getting addicted to mobile- gaming, limiting phone use, refraining from doom scrolling for hours, and also not believeing in random forwarded messages without fact-checking them. He strongly discouraged discontinuing medications based on misinformation.

Through his personal experience and journey and his willingness to share it, with the hope of raising awaresness and inspiring people to adopt a healthier lifestyle, enjoying nature and creating a good social circle, *Father Thomas* transformed a health challenge into an opportunity to promote holistic well-being. His approach demonstrated how such religious personalities can play a vital role in addressing, spiritual, physical and mental well-being.

Tips for Foot Care During Festivals In India and during monsoon season:

- Avoid walking barefoot to temples, mosques, gurudwaras. Wear diabetes- friendly socks. While serving food during langar seva activities in gurudwara wear cushioned diabetic socks while also taking periodic breaks.
- Avoid walking barefoot during festivals like diwali, in order to prevent injuries from broken diyas or fireworks, wear closed breathable footwear to avoid fungal infections from excessive sweating.
- While celebrating festivals like Navratri and Christmas, wear good arch support cushioned footwear and take periodic breaks.
- Inspect your feet before and after the event.
- Moisturize your feet well and get gentle massages.
- Wear water-proof footwear during monsoon season, and keep your feet dry and inspect them especially between toes for signs of fungal infection. Use Antifungal powder if needed.
- During festivals like Onam, dry your feet thoroughly after ceremonial baths.
- While preparing festive sweets and making pookalam (flower-decoration) alternate between standing and sitting position.

CHAPTER SIX

FROM TRADITIONAL TO THERAPEUTIC

"Amid adversity, hidden talents rise, transforming struggles into masterpieces where creativity finds its true expression, turning challenges into triumphs".- Anonymous

While many know *Dharavi as Asia's largest slum* located in Mumbai and for its challenges, it is home to countless skilled artisans and craftsmen who keep India's traditional crafts alive. Masterji, my patient of five years, has been living with diabetes for over twelve years. Amid the narrow lanes and bustling workshops, Masterji's small shop stands as a testament to how traditional skills can adapt to modern health needs. He remains dedicated to leveraging his skills to help others, crafting diabetes-friendly shoes from traditional Indian footwear, although he tackles his condition. Masterji, who has been crafting *Kolhapuri chappals* and *mojris* for decades, is now skilled in diabetic traditional footwear. He meticulously tweaks traditional designs by:

- Adding extra pressure point cushioning
- Providing arch support while maintaining their classical appearance
- For sensitive feet, he uses leather that is both soft and more flexible.

- Ensuring that traditionally narrow designs have sufficient toe space
- Including straps that can be readily adjustable considering foot swelling

Feedback from Patients:

A number of my patients requested Masterji's expertise when word got out about his handcrafted traditional diabetic-friendly footwear.

*Mrs. Ayesha** (name changed), a school teacher, explained how she was able to walk to school without being concerned about blisters thanks to her new customized chappals.

*Mr. Arun** (name chaged), a sales representative, whose job required him to walk a lot, shared how the padded soles eased the strain on his feet after standing and walking for extended periods of time.

*Homemaker Mrs. Anita,**(name changed) stated that she felt more comfortable at social occasions without risking her foot health when she wore *mojris* that appeared authentic, yet safe.

Masterji's joy knew no bounds as his business thrived alongside him feeling deeply humbled and happy by the feedback from other people living with diabetes like himself, that he somehow could contribute and put a smile on their faces as they enjoyed the comfort and aesthetic look, thanks to his skills and his dedication to honoring Indian tradition.

Practical advice while selecting diabetic footwear:

<u>Opt for Soft Materials:</u> To avoid friction against the skin, use soft leather or footwear with memory foam. Avoid hard or rough materials as they may cause blisters or wounds.

<u>Padded Soles:</u> Shoes with cushioned or padded soles put less strain on the feet and are therefore more comfortable to wear for a longer duration.

<u>Seamless Design:</u> Ensure that your footwear is free from excessively tight straps, sharp edges, or seams that may cause irritation to skin.

<u>Proper Fit:</u> Choose footwear that is neither too tight nor too loose. Calluses or injuries can result from poorly fitted shoes.

"Our feet carry us through life, and they deserve the best—comfort, protection, and a touch of tradition".

CHAPTER SEVEN

THE FAMILY CIRCLE

"Just as a single thread cannot hold the fabric, health requires the strength of a family united. In caring for each other, we find the resilience to overcome life's toughest battles".- Anonymous

*Mr. Khan** (name changed), renowned for never taking a day off from his restaurant in the busy *Kurla* area of Mumbai, closed down for two months. Unfortunately, at the age of 68, his dedication to work had taken priority over his health concerns. Despite knowing he had diabetes for the past 10 years, he was not compliant with his medications, lived a sedentary life and was not too concerned about his health as he didn't feel or complain of any symptoms.

A minor cut, however, on his right great toe, which he initially neglected, resulted in a serious infection. This incident became an alarming reminder to him and his family members. The infection had progressed significantly by the time his son brought him to my clinic, requiring me to refer him to a foot surgeon. This ultimately led to the amputation of his right great toe. The whole family was profoundly affected by this event. However, this served as a wake-up call for him and his family to not overlook his condition.

His case shows how challenging it can be for joint families to establish the right equilibrium between cultural traditions and sharing responsibilities. For the *Khan* family, dealing with diabetes required more than just individual care; families must work together, understand one another, and provide moral support to each other.

Key Learning Points from *Mr.Khan's* case:

- Adhere to medication and dietary compliance
- Never overlook even minor foot injuries
- Examine your feet daily
- Regular consultation with your doctor is important
- Family support plays a vital role in managing chronic conditions like diabetes
- Maintain a healthy work-life balance
- Early intervention can help prevent major complications
- Raise awareness about diabetes and its potential complications.

CHAPTER EIGHT

FOOD AND FEET

"Walk with faith, nourish with grace, every challenge is a chance to embrace."- Anonymous

*Anupama Devi** (name changed), had to deal with the difficult decision between reinventing some of her most traditional Indian food recipes or giving them up when she was diagnosed with Type 2 diabetes five years ago. Her condition presented her with a chance for creativity rather than a limitation. According to her, the first idea was to find a way to make her favorite meals healthier while maintaining their essential qualities.

Her home kitchen was set up, and she started experimenting with classic recipes. She incorporated diabetes-friendly spices like fenugreek and turmeric, replaced sugar with stevia and natural fruit purees, and replaced refined flour with almond and chickpea flour. The pivotal moment came during a family get-together when family members were unable to differentiate between her modified and traditional meals. Within days, word spread throughout her locality in Central Mumbai. She grabbed this opportunity with the hope and determination of becoming a self-made entrepreneur at the age of 55. She launched **"Sweet Life,"** an outlet that supplied savory and traditional Indian sweets in diabetic-friendly versions. Today, *Anupama's* kitchen runs a successful operation serving around 50 to 100 regular customers, with the numbers flourishing with each passing day.

As her doctor I'm particularly proud of her as she did not let her diagnosis of diabetes turn into an obstacle, instead, she converted her diagnosis into motivation and an aspirational journey by not giving up her cultural connection to food. Her journey and accomplishment are an example to many of my patients, that it's about finding creative ways to maintain the connection with what we love while taking care of our health.

Insights into Indian Spices:

Turmeric, fenugreek, cinnamon, cardamom, cumin, curry leaves, and black Pepper are some of the most common spices found in every household in India. They have many beneficial effects on people with diabetes. Real-life examples highlight how these spices have helped patients manage their diabetes more effectively, often being used in teas, curries, and as supplements in meals. Many of my patients begin their mornings with a pinch of cinnamon in their tea. The blend and combination of these spices serve as natural remedies and ancestral gifts for healthy living. The key here again is to use everything in moderation alongside medications prescribed by your doctor.

CHAPTER NINE

THE COMMUNITY CONNECT

"The best way to find yourself is to lose yourself in the service of others." – Mahatma Gandhi

Community healthcare workers are at the forefront of raising awareness about numerous health issues, such as, diabetes, in Mumbai and in many other parts of the world. Beyond merely offering healthcare guidance, they encourage communities to take charge of their own well-being. These healthcare providers have made remarkable efforts to raise awareness and enhance knowledge regarding diabetes in Mumbai, a city with a diverse population and bustling neighborhoods.

Developing Healthier Communities in Mumbai:

Local healthcare initiatives in many parts of Mumbai are focusing on educating people about diabetes and its related complications, particularly diabetic foot. *Every 20-30 seconds, a limb is lost due to diabetic foot diseases.* Many residents are unaware of the importance of taking adequate care of their feet, especially those living in underprivileged areas.

Residents are taught how to take good care of their feet. Proper techniques for clipping nails, bathing and drying their feet, and recognizing early signs and symptoms of infection are taught. The local municipal corporation and countless Diabetologists in Mumbai and across India conduct free health camps in an effort to educate the masses and ensure they do not underestimate the diagnosis of diabetes. Efforts are also made by doctors to educate the masses not to fall prey to superstitious beliefs, disregard the diagnosis of diabetes, and delay treatment.

The Role of Religious Events:

Religious gatherings, in addition to celebration and prayer, are often used as platforms to spread awareness. Important messages regarding healthy living are delivered during such events in various places. For example, during community programs healthcare providers and political figures emphasize diabetes as a growing trend in India, it's consequences, and ways to prevent it, in order to maintain their spiritual, physical and emotional well-being without compromising on any aspect. At such gatherings, people are encouraged to get their annual health checkups, and educational materials are provided in an effort to raise more awareness. What makes these programs more successful is that they take place in a familiar and trusted environment, where people already feel a sense of community and support.

CHAPTER TEN

EMPOWERING CHANGE: THE FUTURE OF DIABETES CARE

"It does not matter how slowly you go as long as you do not stop."-Confucius

There are many inspiring stories of individuals and communities who have embraced change and achieved beneficial outcomes as the world continues to battle medical conditions like diabetes, which has reached epidemic proportions and continues to rise rapidly. These tales demonstrate how innovative thinking, traditions, and collaboration, along with pharmaceutical and technological advancements, can all be combined to improve the lives of individuals. These successful cases highlight that the future of diabetes prevention and management is within the sphere of possibility and no longer beyond reach.

Journey from Denial to Empowerment:

*Muskaan**(name changed), a 28-year-old software developer, brushed off her initial diagnosis of diabetes. Like many young adults, she was in denial of her diagnosis, as she had the misconception that diabetes is only a hereditary disease. She continued with her daily routine, not paying much attention to the warning signs her body was signaling. Two weeks later, she walked into my clinic with complaints of fever, a swollen, red, warm left foot, and throbbing pain. Upon questioning and examination, she revealed that she had gone to a foot spa, after which she developed this painful swelling on her foot called Cellulitis, a bacterial infection that had worsened due to uncontrolled blood sugar levels.

Unable to bear the pain and faced with the seriousness of the condition, she willingly accepted starting treatment for diabetes management along with treatment for her foot. Within a week of starting her diabetes medications and antibiotics for her foot infection, she felt much better and decided to take charge of her health while also advocating for diabetes and researching newer modalities and technologies for diabetes management.

She requested to use continuous glucose monitoring - CGM (a small wearable device that continuously tracks blood sugar levels throughout the day and night). She started wearing a smartwatch to track her daily activity and sleep patterns. With the combination of technology, education, and awareness, she transformed not only herself but also her family and peers.

Health Tip:

Use technology to your advantage. Apps and devices like CGM can help you track your blood sugar levels, exercise, and diet and sleep patterns, empowering you to stay on top of your health game and make informed decisions.

People with diabetes should avoid getting foot treatments at unregulated beauty parlors or spas, as poor hygiene can lead to serious infections. Opt for professional foot care services that prioritize safety and specialize in diabetic foot health.

Seeds of Motivation:

After recovering from COVID-19 pneumonia, *Mrs. Aliya** (name changed), was diagnosed with Type 2 diabetes mellitus. This life-altering experience inspired her to transform her small 250-square-foot terrace in the Andheri area of Mumbai into a thriving rooftop kitchen garden. This was her personal endeavor after the COVID scare to indulge in healthy eating and organic farming. Despite Mumbai's challenging weather, she managed to incorporate vertical gardens and recycled containers to grow many different types of vegetables and herbs. The daily gardening routine became a form of mindful exercise, and she enjoyed walking barefoot on the cool morning soil.

One morning, while tending to her garden, a small piece of broken pottery injured her foot, giving her a deep gash, which ultimately led to a week-long hospitalization to recover from the injury. Post this incident, she revamped her routine by wearing thick-soled gardening shoes and gloves and kept the garden pathways clear of debris.

This incident, she shared, taught her, **"Self-care and hobbies must go hand in hand."**. Like many of my patients living with diabetes, she too became an advocate for self-care and raising awareness about diabetes and foot health. She started conducting workshops that led to a dual benefit: teaching people gardening tips while also educating them on how to be mindful of foot health, especially for those living with diabetes. Her experience serves as yet another motivational story, reminding us that we should not limit ourselves due to our illness. **"Sometimes, our biggest mistakes become our best teachers."**

<u>Vision for the Future:</u>

Every day the world is molding and advancing towards technology- which is the future. Many innovations and developments are being made to make life easier and more comfortable for people living with diabetes. Smart footwear is one such cutting-edge technology in the pipeline of advancements. These shoes are equipped with sensors that monitor movement, pressure, and temperature, helping identify foot ulcers or infections early on before they worsen. The goal behind such variations is to prevent the dreaded consequences of diabetic foot disease, which, if overlooked and not treated at the right time, can lead to amputation. If there is a cause for concern with the wearer's foot health, smart shoes notify them so that they can take immediate action. These technologies might become more widespread and integrated into everyday life in the future, potentially revolutionizing foot care.

31

Key Takeaways

Managing diabetes while juggling daily tasks may seem challenging at first, but bear in mind that each tiny step you take today will lead you to a healthier tomorrow.

Start with baby steps: Get moving! Being consistent is the key.

Power Plate: Consider healthier alternatives and be mindful about what you are eating. Make it a habit to read food labels.

Less Stress, Live More: Avoid the rat race! Indulge in activities and hobbies that make you happy.

Early Results, Long-Term Rewards: Get your annual blood checkup done. People living with diabetes should consult their doctor every 2-3 months.

"**Your feet are your foundation**"; therefore, take good care of them, check them every day, and never ignore even minor injuries.

A Heartwarming Message From Your Doctor

Dear Readers,

Diagnosis of diabetes is not the end of the world—**it's a blessing in disguise to take charge of your health.**

I am well aware of the fact that living with diabetes and juggling daily duties can be extremely taxing not just on your physical health but on your mental well-being too. However, I want to remind you that we are walking this path together. Every small action you take towards leading a healthier lifestyle is advancing you towards your best self, hand in hand together.

It's extremely important that you treat yourself with kindness and respect. It's ok to have moments where you don't feel your best and things are not working as planned; it's ok to accept those moments too while still moving forward with hope and courage. Celebrate every victory, no matter how small, and remember, change is possible with determination and effort. You are stronger than you think you are; perhaps you might be a source of encouragement to others while quietly fighting your own battles.

Most IMPORTANTLY, do not compare yourself to others and what you see on social media; it's highly deceiving!!

"Your health is your greatest wealth—nurture it, cherish it, and watch your life flourish."

With warm regards and care,

Dr. Firdous Shaikh

"Like the moon reflects the sun, our
body reflects our care."
Dr. Firdous Shaikh

Testimonials

Competence and Compassion are two opposite ends of the spectrum of a human's "being". Superficially, both have nothing in common. However, to be an effective physician, an efficient physician, and an empathetic physician, one needs to be both competent and compassionate. Both concepts come alive in Dr. Firdous Shaikh's beautifully written book. She speaks of competence, of the ability to pick up subtle cues from the patient's description and demeanor. She shares the feeling of empathy, of being able to place herself not only in the patient's feet but heart as well. Dr Firdous's strong spirituality and robust religiosity speak from each page of the book. She connects the science and study of diabetes with social well-being and spiritual health. By doing so, she fosters a feeling of self-confidence and self-esteem in the reader. This encourages me to work harder at self-care and self-management, thus taking charge of one's health and one's destiny. The author exhibits passion and purpose in her chosen profession and successfully transfers it to the reader. This is what makes Dr. Shaikh a people's physician, a person-centered physician. And this is what makes this book, a people's book, a person-centered book. I have read this book, and reread it and I plan to read it again. It energizes me to work harder at being a good doctor, and at taking better care of people who trust me with their health. To the readers, I entrust this book with confidence and pray that it brings you health and harmony, wellness and well-being.

Dr. Sanjay Kalra, DM
Treasurer, International Society of Endocrinology
Past President, Endocrine Society of India
Bharti Hospital, Karnal, India

Testimonials 2

A very enjoyable and important book on awareness of diabetes foot complications. The content is easy flowing and simple language and analogy have been given by the author Dr. Firdous Shaikh. The entire content was impressive. Thoroughly enjoyed reading the book and definitely a must-read for the general audience to understand how important foot care is in people living with diabetes.

- Dr Shabee Siddiqui (Consultant Diabetologist, Mumbai)

Dr Firdous Shaikh's "Footprints of Wellness " is a beautifully written and impactful guide that bridges the gap between medical advice and cultural relevance. By intertwining practical knowledge with deeply rooted Indian Traditions, she has created a resource that is both accessible and meaningful for the general population. The use of real-life stories, actionable tips, and empathetic guidance makes this book not just an educational tool but a source of hope and empowerment for individuals and families dealing with diabetes. Dr. Shaikh's ability to address the complexities of foot care with simplicity and cultural sensitivity is truly commendable. I am honored to have been a small part of her journey in bringing this valuable contribution to life.

- Dr. Avneesh Khare (Consultant , BrainX AI, USA, Co-Founder , Doctors AI)

Appreciation

I humbly acknowledge and extend my heartfelt gratitude to all my seniors, mentors, and guides who have shaped my professional journey. Your support, wisdom, and encouragement have been the cornerstones of my growth. This entire book may fall short of expressing my thanks to the countless senior doctors who have guided me, provided opportunities, and believed in my potential.

I especially want to thank the following Seniors/ Mentors / Colleagues:

Dr. Abhishek Raha, Dr. Alka Gandhi, Dr. Amit Dey, Dr. Amit Gupta, Dr. Amit Naghate, Dr. Amit Rajput, Dr. Ami Sanghvi, Dr. Anil Bhoraskar, Dr. Anuj Maheshwari, Dr. Ajoy Tewari, Dr. Akash Singh, Dr. Ashish Saxena, Dr. Aswin Mukundan, Dr. Aashna Patil, Dr. Ayaz Ansari, Dr. Avneesh Khare, Dr. Banshi Saboo, Dr. Bharat Saboo, Dr BM Makkar , Dr. Bensley Gonsalves, Dr. Bhavtharini, Dr. Bijay Patni, Dr. Chand Patel, Dr. Deepak Das, Dr. Faraz Farishta, Dr. Fakhra Khan, Dr. Imran Hafizi, Dr. Indumathi Kuberan, Dr. Ishita Sachdev, Dr. Jasmina Vora, Dr. Jaydeep Revale, Dr. Jothydev Kesavadev, Dr. Kavita Rane, Dr. Kashif Shaikh, Dr. Kiran Shah, Dr. Kshitij Bharadwaj, Dr. Lily Rodrigues, Dr. Lotika Purohit, Dr. Mahira Saiyed, Dr. Manoj Chawla, Dr. Mohsin Aslam, Dr. Mudrik Patel, Dr. Muralidharan, Dr. Nadia Phirozmand, Dr. Neelesh Kapoor, Dr. Neeta Shah, Dr. Ninad Gor, Dr. N.K. Singh, Dr. Narsingh Verma, Dr. Noora Pathan, Dr. Pranjali Shah, Dr. Praveen Gangadhara, Dr. Rajesh Kesari, Dr. Rakesh Parikh, Dr. Raka Sheohare, Dr. Riyaz Mohammed, Dr. Ritu Johari, Dr. Rukiya Surya, Dr. Rutul Gokalani, Dr Sanjeev Pathak, Dr. Sajid Ansari, Dr. Saritha Kakani, Dr. Sanjay Kalra, Dr. Seema Bagri, Dr. Shabee Siddiqui, Dr. Shalini Jaggi, Dr. Shefali Karkhanis, Dr. Shivam Verma, Dr. Shruti Gangwani, Dr. Smita Bhatt, Dr. Sunil Gupta, Dr. Suresh Purohit , Dr. Vimal Pahuja, Dr. Vinod Mittal, Dr. Vijay Vishwanathan.

To all the organizations, institutions, and individuals who have contributed in ways big and small, my deepest thanks. If I have unintentionally missed anyone, I sincerely seek your understanding—the list of those who have enriched my journey is truly endless. Thank you all!